Escape from Vesuvius

Story by Julie Mitchell

Illustrated by Vasja Koman

A Moment in History: Vesuvius Erupts!

In 79 AD, Pompeii was a wealthy Italian city, with a population of approximately 20,000. It lay near the Bay of Naples, a short distance from Mount Vesuvius.

Though the mountain had rumbled 17 years earlier, producing an earthquake that damaged Pompeii, the people of Pompeii had no idea that Mount Vesuvius was an active volcano. In the summer of 79 AD, they went about their business, unaware that a full-scale eruption was about to occur.

There were warning signs — tremors rippled through the area, wells and streams dried up, animals became nervous, and ash sifted down over the city. Then, on August 24, Vesuvius erupted, raining hot ashes, stones, and cinders on Pompeii, and filling the air with poisonous fumes.

The inhabitants of Pompeii fled, but at least 2,000 people lost their lives trying to escape. They were sealed inside the buried city.

Contents

Chapter 1
Marcus' Journal

Pompeii
August 18

Cronus, my tutor, was not pleased with my essay on Julius Caesar. He wants me to practice writing, so he suggested that I begin a journal. He has no desire, however, to read this journal. It is simply to be a record of my thoughts and observations, written as though I were speaking to a friend.

I will begin by telling you something about myself. My name is Marcus Gracchus, and I am thirteen. My father is Lucius Gracchus, an oil merchant. My mother is the Lady Octavia Claudia, and I have a younger sister, Lucia. I also have a dog named Ixion.

We live in a large house on a hill overlooking the Bay of Naples, and have ten slaves (including Cronus). My father's cargo ship is anchored in the bay, and we have a small boat, which we use for short trips.

My best friend is Chiro. He is fourteen, and an expert fisherman. Chiro lives farther along the coast, in Herculaneum. Just beyond Herculaneum lies Mount Vesuvius. Father owns many of the olive groves on the slopes of Vesuvius. He is going to inspect them tomorrow. As usual, I will go with him, and I'm allowed to take Ixion. If Chiro isn't busy fishing, perhaps we will be able to spend some time together.

Chapter 2
Warning Signs

Pompeii
August 19

We were lucky — by the time we reached Herculaneum, Chiro already had a full haul of fish, so he was free for the afternoon.

Chiro, Ixion, and I accompanied Father to the olive groves, then set off to explore the mountainside.

We climbed higher than we ever had before — up beyond the olive groves, orchards, and vineyards, to where the woods begin. Then we rested, and I noticed a peculiar thing — the ground beneath me felt very warm.

I was about to mention this to Chiro when something disturbing happened. The earth began to shake! It felt as though the grassy floor of the woods had become liquid, like the sea, and we had been helplessly cast adrift on its heaving surface. Ixion barked. I tried to go to him, but I was unable to stand.

Then, just as suddenly as it had begun, the shaking stopped. "What was that?" I asked Chiro.

"A tremor," he answered. "We've had a lot of them lately, but my father says they're nothing to worry about."

Although I admired Chiro's confidence, I was a little unsettled by the tremor, so I mentioned it to Father during the journey home. Like Chiro's father, he said it was nothing to worry about. I hope he's right, but I suspect that he was less concerned with the earth tremor than with the condition of his olive groves. Some of the wells on Mount Vesuvius have dried up, and the stream he relies on for irrigation has ceased flowing. The olives are a good size, but without water from the stream, their quality will suffer.

It was nightfall when we reached home, and Lucia greeted us excitedly. Mother's plans for tomorrow night's dinner party were well under way, and Helen (our cook) had already made the special seasoning my sister loves — a mixture of dried figs, honey, and bay leaves.

I was going to warn Lucia not to steal too much of the seasoning, when suddenly a tremor passed through the house. Lucia screamed, and I managed to calm her, though I did not feel the least bit calm myself.

I looked down at the floor in our entrance hall and noticed that the tremor had damaged the mosaic near the door. The mosaic depicts a wild boar, but some of the tiles near the boar's nose had been shaken loose. I picked one up and passed it to Father. He looked concerned for a moment. Then he passed it back to me, saying nothing.

9

Chapter 3
The Streets of Pompeii

Pompeii
August 20

It was already hot when I awoke this morning, and the house was full of activity. Mother had set the slaves to cleaning, running errands, and cooking, in preparation for the banquet.

I found her in the summer dining room, supervising the cleaning. "Have you seen your sister?" she asked. But before I could answer, she added, "I hope she's not getting underfoot in the kitchen. Go and check, would you please, Marcus?"

Lucia was, of course, in the kitchen, her mouth full of fig seasoning. "Doesn't everything look wonderful?" she said.

I had to admit that it did. On the table before us lay an amazing array of food: flamingos' tongues with fish livers; leaves stuffed with nuts and raisins; assorted shellfish and salads; a seasoned ham wrapped in pastry; and on the largest platter of all, pieces of boiled pig, arranged to look like a goose, surrounded by thrushes rolled in flour.

While Lucia and I admired the first two courses, Helen and three other slaves bustled about, preparing the third: cheesecakes sprinkled with poppy seeds; animals made from fruit and marzipan; and "ova mellita," a dish of honeyed eggs.

"We'd better go, Lucia," I said. "Mother doesn't want us getting in the way."

In fact, Mother didn't want **anyone** to upset her dinner preparations. After lunch she suggested that Father go to the Forum baths. (She told him he needed to relax, but we all knew she just wanted to get him out of the house!) Then she told Lucia and me to take Ixion for a walk.

As we walked through the streets of Pompeii, I noticed how still and quiet everything was. Not a breath of air stirred a leaf. Not a seagull cried overhead. Even Ixion seemed quieter than usual.

Farther along the street, Enzo, the bronzesmith, was securing a cartload of his wares. His horse stood motionless, but its ears were pointing upward, as though listening for something. In the heavy silence of the afternoon, I called a greeting to Enzo. He looked up and waved to me.

Then suddenly, all was chaos.

Enzo's horse reared, upending the cart and spilling lamps and lanterns onto the road. There was a loud rumble, and the pavement heaved, causing us to stagger around. A woman nearby cried out as a roof tile fell and cut her forehead. Lucia squealed with fright, and Ixion turned in circles, whimpering.

Fear consumed me. I thought the ground would crack open at any moment!

We were too frightened to continue our walk, so we hurried home. Mother told us the tremor had been felt there, too. "I'm sure it's nothing serious, though," she said. "There's no need to worry."

The banquet went ahead as planned, and even at this late hour I can hear the laughter of my parents and their guests.

Why are they not afraid?

Chapter 4
Cronus' Tale

Pompeii
August 21

This morning I told Cronus about my fears. I had hoped for reassurance, but instead he launched into a detailed account of the earthquake that damaged Pompeii, Naples, and Herculaneum 17 years ago.

"The earth shook violently," he said. "It heaved up Pompeii's water pipes and ripped them apart. Columns broke and statues fell, and several of the villas and smaller houses collapsed, burying people inside."

Cronus shook his head. "Some of those people were my friends," he said sadly. Then, spreading his arms wide, he showed me how the earth had opened up and swallowed 600 sheep!

I listened to his account with growing horror, then I asked him if he thought such a thing could happen again.

"It's unlikely, Marcus," he said. "It was a rare event — so rare that the citizens of Pompeii spent a great deal of time and money restoring the city to its former glory. They wouldn't have done so if they believed it could be destroyed by another earthquake."

The citizens of Pompeii might have been confident when they rebuilt the city, but I wonder if they feel so confident now.

Chapter 5

Fear

Pompeii
August 22

The earth tremors continue, and there are cracks in the walls of our house. The slaves are busy repairing them, but no sooner is one crack concealed than another appears.

Father sailed for Misenum this afternoon. He is taking a cargo of oil to the naval base there. I accompanied him to the harbor, and while the oil was being loaded, I noticed the pack animals behaving strangely. The horses, mules, and oxen were skittish — shying and rolling their eyes.

The seagulls, too, behaved in an unusual manner. Instead of wheeling above us, screeching at each other, they gathered silently on the shore. Then, as one, they flew away.

Pompeii
August 23

Ixion is acting strangely. He has been pacing from room to room all day. He seems very nervous — and he is not the only one. Some of our neighbors have gone in search of safer ground. Two of our slaves have run away and Mother is furious. She says they are cowards, but I don't blame them for being afraid.

Lucia is having nightmares. I'm not sleeping well, either. A short time ago, I went for a walk in the garden. When I came back inside, I noticed that I was covered with a fine layer of gray powder. At first I thought it was dust, but when I brushed it from my skin, I recognized the smell of ash.

What does this mean?

Chapter 6
Eruption!

Misenum
August 24

Though I am still trembling, I will try to write down today's events as clearly as possible. Late this morning, Mother, Lucia, Cronus, and I went to the Forum of Pompeii. We left Ixion at home, because he's been so unsettled. Mother took Lucia to the Building of Eumachia to look at woven cloth, while Cronus began to teach me about architecture.

We went to a number of buildings, where Cronus pointed out differences in style. Then he suggested that we visit the Temple of Isis, in order to study its columns.

The temple was a short distance from the Forum. As we approached it, we heard the low rumble of yet another tremor passing through the city.

The sanctuary of Isis was deserted when we entered. "The priests are having their lunch," Cronus whispered to me. "It will be another hour before they perform their next service."

Suddenly, there was a deafening **CR-A-A-CK**! The floor lurched. Cronus gripped my arm and hurried me outside.

The columns on the temple grounds rocked
unsteadily, and I did not want to pass beneath
them. I hesitated, then followed Cronus. I
glanced back and saw the priests of Isis bolting
from the temple. One leaped safely down the
steps. But another halted for a moment, and was
crushed as the column nearest him fell.

"This way!" Cronus shouted, propelling me
safely into an alleyway.

We headed back the way we had come, often losing our footing as the street buckled. On either side of the alley, buildings swayed, showering us with bricks and tiles. The air filled with a stench like that of rotten eggs, and the sun's light left us.

Ash began to fall, and stones — some as big as a man's fist — pelted down upon us. "What's happening?" I cried.

"I don't know!" Cronus shouted above the clatter. "Keep running! We have to find your mother and Lucia!"

At last we reached the Forum. I couldn't believe what I saw. Amid broken columns and fallen statues, people scrambled about, screaming as they sought shelter. Fires from overturned lamps lit the agonized faces of those who had been hit by chunks of solid rock. And beyond all this, Vesuvius, its summit open like a red mouth, had become a roaring cannon, sending a gigantic column of speckled white fire into the sky.

"All these years, we thought Vesuvius was just a mountain," said Cronus. "But it isn't **just** a mountain — it's a volcano. And it's erupting!" He turned to me. "We have to leave here as quickly as possible," he said. Then he swiftly guided me across the Forum to the Building of Eumachia.

23

We found Mother and Lucia huddled together in a doorway. "Quickly!" Cronus ordered, snatching up some nearby cushions. "Hold these over your heads and follow me!"

"But it's not safe anywhere!" Mother protested. "Where can we go?"

"To the harbor," Cronus said. "We'll take the boat and head for Misenum."

We ran all the way to the harbor. Thank goodness the pier was still standing. Our boat was full of stones, but it was not damaged. Cronus and I threw the stones into the heaving sea. Then we helped Mother and Lucia aboard, cast off, and sailed for Misenum.

It was a long and treacherous journey. We were almost swamped several times. Pebbles rained down upon us. Hot cinders set the sail on fire, and we were forced to row. In the unnatural darkness, I feared that we would lose our way. Misenum, and Father, seemed very far away.

By the time we reached calmer waters, true night was approaching. In the distance, lightning flashed around the fiery column of Vesuvius, and I hoped that Chiro and his family were safe. I thought about those we had left behind in Pompeii — Helen and the other slaves, our relatives, and friends. Were they safe somewhere?

And what about Ixion? Was he safe? Or was he lying under a pile of rubble, injured and in pain? The image was too much to bear, and tears welled up in my eyes.

Cronus must have noticed that I was upset. "Marcus," he said gently, "concentrate on rowing. Worrying won't help."

I took his advice, bending my will to the task. And finally, on the horizon, I saw the lights of Misenum.

The beach was aglow with lanterns. When we reached the shallows, uniformed sailors ran toward us through the water. As they towed us in, I scanned the shore, hoping to spot Father. But I could not see him anywhere.

I heard someone calling our names. And suddenly, Father was in our boat!

I had never seen him cry, but he sobbed unashamedly as he embraced us all — even Cronus.

Then, picking up Lucia and holding her tightly, Father said to Cronus, "Thank you for saving my family. As of this day, I make you a free man."

He reached for the slave belt that marked Cronus as a piece of our property. Then he took it from Cronus's waist, and threw it into the sea.

Cronus watched the slave belt he had worn for years disappear beneath the water. Then he turned to Father, his own eyes brimming. "Thank you, Lucius Gracchus," he said solemnly. "I never thought I'd see the day when I'd be free again."

I was filled with joy. And when Chiro and his family were towed to shore in an old fishing boat an hour later, I thought my heart would burst.

Chapter 7
New Horrors

Misenum
August 25

For hours, Chiro and I watched the bright fury of Vesuvius reaching skyward. Then, quite suddenly, the enormous column of fire collapsed. Rivers of glowing lava began to flow down the sides of the volcano, and we knew that Herculaneum would be destroyed.

Grateful that we were safe with our families at the naval base, Chiro and I retired to our beds. But the early hours of this morning brought new horrors.

A series of violent earth tremors shook the city, and as we all fled into the countryside, Vesuvius issued a dreadful black cloud, which descended upon the sea and the land. We were enveloped by it, and day became night. Ashes fell so thickly that we continually shook them off for fear that they would bury us.

Eventually the nightmare ended and pale daylight appeared. As we returned to Misenum, Father vowed that we would never be in danger again. He proposed that we move to Rome, far away from Vesuvius. He offered Cronus a handsome salary if he would come with us and continue to be my tutor. Cronus agreed, and Father had the cargo ship made ready.

Tomorrow, at first light, we sail for Rome.

Chapter 8
The Buried City

Bay of Naples
September 16

Three weeks have passed since my last journal entry, but so much has happened that it has been difficult to find time to write.

When we reached Rome, we heard rumors that Pompeii had disappeared under a layer of solid ash. The idea was so shocking that Mother refused to believe it. She insisted that we sail back home, so that we could see for ourselves. Father was not sure that we should go, but Mother was determined, and he eventually agreed. So we boarded the ship once more.

Unfortunately, the rumors proved to be true. Pompeii was buried under an expanse of solidified ash. It was a wasteland, broken only by the very tops of the Forum's pillars, arches, and statues.

Standing on a hill above the entombed city, I tried to discern where our house was. I wondered about Helen, and our other slaves. I hoped that they had escaped. I hardly dared to think about what might have happened to Ixion. Had he died alone, and in pain? Was he buried somewhere beneath the ash?

That last thought made my eyes water, and as we made our way back to the seashore, I tried to put it out of my head.

It was no good though. I found myself counting up everything Vesuvius had taken from me — my home, our slaves, relatives, and friends. That it had taken our dog as well, seemed too much to bear.

Overwhelmed with grief, I sat on the beach and cried, while Father prepared the light boat that would take us back to our ship.

Something nudged my arm, but I was so upset that I didn't notice. Then I felt hot breath on my cheek. I looked up, and couldn't believe my eyes. There — dusty, thin, and too weak to bark — was Ixion! Somehow, he had survived.

I threw my arms around him, and fresh tears rolled down my face. But I was no longer crying over what had been taken from me. I was crying over what had been given back.